Cooking SCHOOL

French Food

SARA GILBERT

CREATIVE EDUCATION & CREATIVE PAPERBACKS

Published by Creative Education and Creative Paperbacks
P.O. Box 227, Mankato, Minnesota 56002 • Creative Education
and Creative Paperbacks are imprints of The Creative Company
www.thecreativecompany.us

Design and production by Christine Vanderbeek
Printed in the United States of America

Photographs by Corbis (VINCENT KESSLER/Reuters, Poplis,
Paul/the food passionates), Dreamstime (Quentin Bargate,
Ppy2010ha, Spaxia), Getty Images (Todd Bates), iStockphoto
(Ursula Alter, naelnabil, Dirk Richter), Shutterstock (area381,
Artmim, Jiri Hera, HLPhoto, llaszlo, Denis Kichatof, Vitaly Korovin,
jan kranendonk, marco mayer, NEGOVURA, nrt, pogonici, Evlakhov
Valeriy, Visionsi, VolkOFF-ZS-BP, Yganko, zhekoss)

Library of Congress Cataloging-in-Publication Data
Gilbert, Sara. • French food / by Sara Gilbert. • p. cm. —
(Cooking school) • Summary: An elementary introduction to the
relationship between cooking and French culture, the effect of
local agriculture on the diets of different regions, common dishes
such as ratatouille, and recipe instructions.
Includes bibliographical refer-
ences and index. • ISBN
978-1-60818-502-3 (*hard-
cover*) • ISBN 978-
1-62832-096-1 (*pbk*)
1. Cooking, French—Juvenile
literature. 2. Food—France—
Juvenile literature. I. Title.
TX719.G535 2015
641.5944—dc23
2014002297

CCSS: RI.1.1, 2, 3, 5, 6, 7;
RI.2.1, 2, 3, 5, 6, 7; RI.3.1,
3, 5, 7; RF.1.1; RF.2.3, 4;
RF.3.3

First Edition
9 8 7 6 5 4 3 2 1

Table of Contents

Delicious Foods

People cook because they need to feed their families. But cooking *nutritious* foods is also fun. In France, cooks enjoy creating foods that taste good!

Tarte tatin is an upside-down baked dessert made with fruit.

Fancy Meals

French food is known for being fancy, looking pretty, and tasting good. French cooks like to say "Bon appétit," which means, "Enjoy your meal!"

French cooks use sauces to add flavor and color.

Taste of France

Stews and soups are common in northern France. The *climate* is cool there. People eat a lot of seafood such as lobster.

Seafood can be added to rich soups or eaten on its own.

The city of Paris is famous for fancy restaurants. People can order *gourmet* foods like escargot, which is the French word for "snail."

Escargot are often cooked in butter with spices and herbs.

Many cheeses are made in the French Alps. They are used in fondue, a hot dipping sauce for bread.

Some French cheese is soft (left), while hard cheeses are melted.

People in the south of France like to eat a fish soup called bouillabaisse (*BOOL-yuh-base*). They also like ratatouille (*rat-uh-TOO-ee*), a flavorful vegetable dish.

Bouillabaisse (left) and ratatouille need fresh ingredients.

French Bread

Bread and cheese are necessary parts of the French *diet*. Many people buy fresh bread daily and eat it with every meal.

In France,

French toast

is made with bread that is stale, or no longer fresh.

INGREDIENTS

1 cup milk

2 eggs

1 teaspoon vanilla extract

¼ teaspoon ground cinnamon

1 loaf French bread

syrup, powdered sugar, or strawberry slices for serving

DIRECTIONS

1. Stir together 1 cup milk, 2 eggs, 1 teaspoon vanilla extract, and ¼ teaspoon ground cinnamon.

2. Coat a frying pan with cooking spray and, with an adult's help, heat the pan.

3. Cut a loaf of French bread into 1-inch slices. Dip each slice into the egg and milk mixture to coat both sides.

4. Place the bread on the frying pan. Cook for a minute, then flip. Serve with syrup, powdered sugar, or strawberry slices.

Fondue

can be made with cheese, hot oil, or even chocolate!

INGREDIENTS

1 cup milk

1 tablespoon chopped garlic

1 pound grated Monterey Jack cheese

2 tablespoons flour

bread cubes, vegetables, or apple or pear slices for dipping

DIRECTIONS

1. Heat 1 cup milk and 1 tablespoon chopped garlic in a saucepan or fondue pot for 3 minutes.

2. Stir together 1 pound *grated* Monterey Jack cheese and 2 tablespoons flour. Stir the cheese into the milk. Keep stirring until mixture is smooth.

3. Use a fork to carefully dip bread cubes, fresh vegetables, or apple or pear slices into the cheese.

Ratatouille

is a popular main dish in France.

INGREDIENTS

1 tablespoon oil

1 tablespoon chopped garlic

1 large eggplant

Parmesan cheese

zucchini

onion

tomato

salt and pepper

DIRECTIONS

1. With an adult's help, preheat the oven to 350 °F and coat a small baking dish with cooking spray. Heat 1 tablespoon oil in a frying pan. Add 1 tablespoon chopped garlic.

2. Slice a large eggplant and add it to the frying pan. Let it cook for about 10 minutes, then spread it in the baking dish. Sprinkle Parmesan cheese over it. Then layer slices of zucchini, onion, and tomato over the top. Sprinkle with salt and pepper, and top with more cheese.

3. Bake for 45 minutes or until the vegetables are soft. Bon appétit!

Glossary

climate the general long-term weather conditions in an area

diet the foods a person usually eats

gourmet describing fine food or a restaurant that serves fine food

grated cut into small shreds

nutritious healthy and good for you

stews dishes of meat and vegetables cooked slowly in liquid

Read More

Blaxland, Wendy. *I Can Cook! French Food*. Mankato, Minn.: Smart Apple Media, 2011.

Crocker, Betty. *Betty Crocker Kids Cook!* Minneapolis: Betty Crocker, 2007

Low, Jennifer. *Kitchen for Kids*. New York: Whitecap Books, 2010.

Websites

http://www.pbs.org/food/theme/cooking-with-kids/
Find easy recipes to try by yourself or with an adult's assistance.

http://www.foodnetwork.com/cooking-with-kids/package/index.html
Learn to cook with celebrity chefs on the website of television's Food Network.

Note: Every effort has been made to ensure that the websites listed above are suitable for children, that they have educational value, and that they contain no inappropriate material. However, because of the nature of the Internet, it is impossible to guarantee that these sites will remain active indefinitely or that their contents will not be altered.

Index